The Phoenix Living Poets

OLD MOVIES

OLD MOVIES

and other poems

by

JOHN COTTON

CHATTO AND WINDUS

THE HOGARTH PRESS

1971

Published by
Chatto and Windus Ltd
with The Hogarth Press Ltd
42 William IV Street
London W.C.2

★

Clarke, Irwin & Co. Ltd
Toronto

Distributed in the United States of America
by Wesleyan University Press

ISBN: 0 8195 7031 1

ISBN 0 7011 1689 7

Printed in Great Britain by
William Lewis (Printers) Ltd
Cardiff

To Peggy and the boys

Acknowledgements are due to the editors of the following periodicals and anthologies, in which certain of the poems have appeared.

The Aylesford Review, The Critical Survey, Encounter, Enigma, Form, New Measure, The Observer, Outposts, Phoenix, The Poetry Review, Priapus, Solstice, Speak (B.B.C.), The Transatlantic Review, Tribune, Workshop 2.

The Borestone Mountain Poetry Award Anthology 'Best Poems of 1966' (Pacific Books, U.S.A.); The P.E.N. Anthology 'New Poems 1967' (Hutchinsons); The Poet and Printer Anthology 'Five Quiet Shouters'; 'Best S.F. of 1969' (G.P. Putnam's); Poetry: Introduction 1 (Faber & Faber).

The Barrow Poets, B.B.C. Schools' Programmes and B.B.C. T.V.

Contents

PIGS *(Four ways of looking at)*
To Westacre Belle and Prestatyn Lucy

Scrubbed pink
They look the most naked of animals,
Except for the coarse hair,
Almost colourless and seen close to.
With ears like awnings over their small eyes,
They root with their blunt and specially
Gristled noses, their legs almost
Ridiculously delicate
For all that warmth and fertility.
Twelve or thirteen a time, is it?
She grunts to let them know they can feed.
Few are allowed to reach full size:
Boiled down they make excellent lard.

The delicate colouring
And firmness of line
Remind one
Of a water colour by Durer.
As St. John and Socrates
Were at pains to point out:
Nature is always
Imitating art.

Domesticated since neolithic times
They are still indifferent to man.
Clumsy, sometimes bad tempered,
They can crack a leg by rolling on it
Or smother a litter. And those jaws,
Like clapper boards, that open as if
The face was falling apart,
Can make short work of a piglet
Or an arm.

9

In Chinese ideography,
A roof with a pig under it
Means home.

Contents

OLD MOVIES

How I loved those old movies
they would show in the Roxys
and Regals amongst all that
gilt plaster, or in the Bijou
flea-pits smelling of Jeyes.
The men sleek haired and suited,
with white cuffs and big trilbies,
their girls all pushovers,
wide-eyed with lashes
like venus fly traps and their
clouds of blonde candyfloss
for hair. Oh those bosoms, hips
and those long long legs
I never saw in daylight!
And their apartments,
vast as temples,
full of unused furniture,
the sideboards bending with booze,
and all those acres of bed!
She, in attendance, wearing
diaphanous, but never quite
diaphanous enough, nightwear.
And their lives!
Where the baddies only,
if not always, stopped one,
and they loved and loved
and never ended up married.
Every time I get a whiff
of that disinfectant
I feel nostalgic.

LABUAN 1946

We pull ashore from a craft

anchored in the still bay,

the slack slap of waters

at the clinkered prow

before we ground to wade

through the shallows

to the now deserted beach:

To our right

the angle-ironed shells of landing craft,

                                          above

the broad blades of palms

cut dark slices from a sun bleached sky;

the sun sucking, after rain,

vegetation from dank earth.

Just up the beach, surprising,

a handful of alien white slabs

all but submerged in tall grasses.

We stoop to read:

> *Colour Sgt.*
> *Adam Sutherland, Royal*
> *Marines, Killed in Action*
> *Against Balinese Pirates*
> *Eighteen-forty-seven*

and time is the least distance.

The burial party,

their boat beached hard by ours,

the pipe clay, the blue,

the sailors' straw hats,

the parting shot

that silence is to overlay.

Sounds carrying,

only that of the sea remains,

while we stand,

sharing that frisson of curiosity

prompted

by the indifference of untried places

before they left him.

13

ALLOTMENTS

Here, where the best crop is stones,
between the churchyard and the railway,
are the allotments, divided
by grass strips, where turnips, white,
hard, round, compete with pebbles,
sparse cabbage struggles towards spring,
and plastic, like prayer flags,
scares birds from half planted rows
as regular as rails.
All this care for so little.

The churchyard grows its stones too,
each plot well marked: *In Loving
Memory* or *Safe with Jesus,*
sparrows darting amongst them –
a fresh one gaudy with tributes,
and one, neglected, small, *for
Thomas Jeremy aged three,*
its metal urn rust eaten –
the knapped flint of the church,
close by, still growing.

PHILOCTETES

Below a sky bleached by the sun,
The beasts and trees my present care,
Abandoned, treacherously undone,
I king this island in despair:
Yet they'll have need of me.

My wound, the putrefying flesh,
The reasons given at the time;
Yet does not one of them confess
The actual nature of my crime?
That they had need of me,

To lead them, where they would not lead
Themselves, and there received the blow
That festers like my mind and feeds
Their sickness that will surely grow
Because they needed me,

And others like me, hard, strong-armed,
Unloved, my brothers in those tasks
That man disdains, his ways demand,
So in necessity he asks
Those others and his need of me.

So here reviled I still keep fast
My bow in readiness, my pain,
The true one, knowing at the last,
In spite of all, I'm used again
When they have need of me.

There's no escape, my purpose and
This island's coast keep me on call,
I wait, I shoot, I roam the sand,
And nurse a hatred that is all
Their need of me.

TOAD

Squat, granular skinned,
the shape and colour of clods,
this stationary predator —
as still as a sadhu in contemplation —
his hinged tongue at the ready,
is all utility built
to his coppery periscope eyes
and high placed nostrils.
His shape, stillness and warts
designed for survival,
as the icey fires of his heart:
the night his day,
the rain his moving time.
Evolved in remote carbon —
iferous times he would seem
as remote from us.
Even his mating is simple,
his croak reserved to indicate whereabouts,
a firm grip under the arms
with his four fingered hands
for a straightforward spawning.
Yet those hands, used,
at other times, for stuffing in food,
are like those of a manikin.
And like us he lives between two worlds,
his neither fish nor mammal,
ours angel nor beast;
and, as with us,
his warts are part of him.

THE WESTERNERS

Were they the real Protestant heroes,
Those Westerners of the screen,
Tall in the saddle and journeying
Into the far country,
Alone and seeking their own salvation,
Owing allegiance to none of the big outfits?
All the trappings of hagiology were theirs:
The stern unwritten code;
The self-denial of the long nights
In the wilderness of the Californian Desert;
The Magdalenes of the saloons,
In their frills and high-heeled boots
And the Hays permitted daring
Of decolletage,
For whom they would stand
With backs to the long bar mirror
Waiting for him who would cast the first stone,
As quick on the draw
As the angel that arrested Abraham.
Theirs, too, the hair-splitting theology
Of murder and self-defence;
Though at the end there was no casuistry,
On the day of the inevitable
Long walk down Main Street,
Where good and evil
Shot it out.

LANDSCAPE CARDIGANSHIRE

Tokens of failure?
The bleached and hollow
Narrow skull of a sheep,

The empty fold and
The dry-stone cottage
Reduced to scree. Yet look,

In the distance are
Sheep, white like maggots
Feeding on the hillside,

And rhubarb, in what
Was once a garden,
Pushes up each summer.

As when I am gone,
And you lie alone
In a bed soon to be

Filled by another.
It's individuals
That perish.

CAMP DOCTOR

I did not make the orders,
My duty was to give them.
Besides, the sorting apart,
I would try to keep away.
There was the smell, like roasting,

The burning of mattresses,
Acrid, sweet, at the same time,
I wanted no part of it.
Though there was always the smoke
From chimneys to remind us.

I only did injections,
Perhaps five or six hundred,
I cannot be sure; we were,
As I said, under orders.
Naturally there were some

I felt sorry for: their eyes
A liquid vacancy of
Despair, the ribs like washboards.
Sometimes I spoke to children
(Reassuringly) before

They were taken. Though it's surprising
What you get used to.
Of course I took care to keep
Most strictly to my duty.
I had a wife and children,

Was good to my dog. I'm not
An imaginative man.

REPORT BACK

"O dark dark dark. They all go into the dark,
The vacant interstellar spaces"
T.S. Eliot: *East Coker*

Galactic probe seven-thousand and four
Reports an uneventful journey, free
From any serious meteoric collisions.
Geological and radiation
Surveys are now being prepared, though our first
Instrumentation suggests little, if
Any, difficulty in setting up
The usual research apparatus.

> *And looking into the void*
> *From the far edge of our empire*
> *We see the next galaxy*
> *A rapidly receding*
> *Thumb-smudge of light in a mid-*
> *Night violet sky pierced by the*
> *Dead-lights of a handful of planets,*
> *Red-tinged and steady like the*
> *Eyes of disappointed lovers,*
> *And our perspective's gone.*

Gravity repulsion is now reduced
To a minimum, while preliminary
Spectrascopic analysis suggests
Possible vegetation, though we seem,
At present, on what is clearly a desert.

> *Pock-marked with small craters*
> *To the edge of a ragged*
> *Horizon, and long-shadowed*
> *In what passes for a moon*
> *On the galactic periphary,*

20

Here is an austere beauty,
Barren, uncompromising,
Like that which must have been
Experienced by men
On the ice-caps and deserts
As they once existed on earth
Before their urbanization.
Harsh and unambiguous
It throws, as it were, a man
Into himself. Is this what
The early poets wrote about?

Our first extra-craft exploration has
Returned with specimens, one of which may
Be a new mineral. We are working
On the uranium breakdown now.
We have found, also, what appear to be
Pebbles, which suggest the action of seas,
Suggesting life, if not now, at some time.
With the spectrascopic analysis
This could prove most interesting. We will
Begin work radio-gravitation
Project immediate first light. Meanwhile,
We are now occupied with lab. work as
It is eighty hours until the next 'dawn'.
The darkness, as expected, is intense.

O the dark, the deep hard dark
Of these galactic nights!
Even the planets have set
Leaving it slab and impenetrable,
As dark and directionless
As those long nights of the soul
The ancient mystics spoke of.
Beyond there is nothing,
Nothing we have known or experienced.

21

It is such a dark
To be lost in which a man
Might, perhaps, find himself.

Excessive hyperwarp has set up
A fault in our auxiliary booster,
Could you contact the depot-ship asking
To send a supply-cruiser with a spare?
And, while they are at it, some playing-cards
Or a set of Galaxtopoly with
A few of the latest girlie magazines.
Anything to kill the time.

If a man could stare out
Such a darkness and endure,
In such a darkness a man
Might, perhaps, find himself,
Scoured to the quick
In the timeless sands of the void.

Anything, as I said, to kill the time.

THE SEAFARER

(from the Old English)

I'll tell you the truth about myself
of travels and the hardships I've suffered,
misery endured and my experience on ships,
of countless anxieties and the fearful rolling of the waves.
Often I kept the night watch, comfortless
on the ship's prow as it tossed close to the cliffs.
Harassed by cold and hunger, my feet frost-bitten,
I complained of the misery that cut into my heart
and my sea-weary soul. He who gets rich on shore
can't understand how worn out with worry
and stiff with cold I stuck out that winter,
exiled and far from my mates . . . .
The hail flew in showers, I could hear nothing
except the pounding sea, the ice-cold waves
and, at times, the cry of water birds.
Not for me the pleasures of a joke and a jar;
but only the storm-lashed cliffs, the screech of gulls
and the cries and screams of birds
whose names I'm not sure of,
and never a companion to cheer me.
He who lives a soft life in the city,
enjoying himself, complacent and flushed with booze,
will never know what I, often dead tired,
have to put up with at sea when night darkens,
the snow comes in from the north, the deck freezes hard,
and a hoary harvest of hail begins to fall.

In spite of all this, my nature is such
I'll go to sea again, risk the rising
surge of the waters. I just don't seem able,
when the fit is on me, to resist the urge to travel,
to visit strange lands and their distant peoples.
Yet there is no man on earth so proud,

so remarkably gifted, so foolhardy
or so daring, nor God so good to him
that he cannot be apprehensive about his seafaring
or what Fate has got up his sleeve for him.
He doesn't care about the pleasures of music,
riches or women, the ways of the world
or anything save the vastness of the oceans.
He who has the sea in his blood
is always restless to set sail.

In spring the world begins to stir,
fields flourish, woods flower
and even cities become beautiful.
All this is a signal to the restless minded man
to sail far on the depths of the ocean.
Yet, at the same time, the mournful voice
of the cuckoo, the herald of summer,
brings a certain sadness to the mind.
The prosperous landsman cannot know
what the deep sea sailor has to put up with;
nevertheless I can't shake off
that unsatisfied longing to sail
far over the Earth to the demesne of the whales.
I'm one with that lone-bird that calls
irresistibly, and sharpens my longing
to sail again on those oceans
where the only roads are the whales'.

The fact is, to me there are
more lasting joys than this dead fleeting
life on earth. I can't believe
the things of this world are lasting.
Only death is certain, though by disease,
old age or violence one can never be sure
until the time comes. It is the lasting praise
of those who survive us that is the best

24

a man can strive for on this earth.
That bravery against both the spite of the devil
and the malice of enemies is what lives
in the respect of those who come after
and is honoured by angels. It is in such joy
that the brave can find immortality.

The time has gone
when there was honour in the Kingdoms of the earth.
Kings, emperors and those other rich patrons
are not as they used to be when between them
they performed great and glorious deeds
and lived in honoured splendour.
All this excellence is now past,
now lesser men possess the earth
enjoying it by their labours. Great men are few
and what is worthwhile ages and withers,
as with everyman in this world
when old age comes, when cheeks lose their colour
and he mourns the coming of grey hairs
and those noble friends who, already,
have been buried in the earth.

Then, once his own life has gone
the flesh feels neither pleasure nor pain,
the hands not stir to touch nor the mind to thought.
Though a man, when he buries his brother
with the dead, covers his grave with gold
and other treasures he would have him
take with him, gold hoarded in this life
is no consolation to the soul
alone in the presence of God.

25

LOVE SONG

There will come a time
When all there is to be said
will be said.

When only the fingers' ends
And the raw nerve of our love
will articulate.

There will come a time
When all there is to be dead
Will be dead.

When only the dust and
The unspeakable in the beginning word
Will remain.

Yet still the worm nags,
And old bones grind
For a new song.

AUTUMNAL

Free from the screeching night omens
Of owls, I walk alone the length
Of this oozing autumn morning,
The grasses mist drenched, the briars rich
In the congealed gouts of their hips.
Feet squelch in the soft rot of leaves
Where in the cold aisles of the trees
Fungi construct out of the mould
Their unlit ephemeral selves.

Approaching the trees, cathedral
Branched their great trunks isolated
In mist heavy with the incense
Of decay, I touch their dark moss
Dank bark to know them in their fall,
Leaf scars sealed, locked in essential
Loneliness against that season
When tenacity is all, and
To each its own preparation.

BRACKEN

Vegetable phoenix,
the bracken, out of the dry
combustible debris of
their predecessors, thrust up
green hoops, later to straighten
as they push towards the sun.
The young fronds tight and foetus-
like, each pair's slow unfolding
(measurable only by days)
maintains an exact balance
until the delicately
feathered leaf wings are fully
extended to hover like birds.
Heath fires can set bracken back,
not destroy them. Cut them back
or attempt to suppress them,
as with thoughts or emotions,
they will reappear. Their reserves
are deeper. Similarly,
note how once they take a hold
little else flourishes.
Stand still a moment, can't you
feel them pushing, pushing
to the surface?

PUMPKINS

At the end of the garden,
Across the litter of weeds and grass cuttings
The pumpkin spreads its coarse,
Bristled, hollow-stemmed lines,
Erupting in great leaves
Above flowers
The nobbly and prominent
Stigmas of which
Are like fuses
Waiting to be set by bees.

When, like a string
Of yellow mines
Across the garden,
The pumpkins will smoulder
And swell,
Drawing the combustion from the sun
To make their own.

At night I lie
Waiting for detonations,
Half expecting
To find the garden
Cratered like a moon.

OLD BOOKSELLER

First there were books
    and after books came art,
these were his life
    as if he were a part
of the shop he ran,
    spending his days
in those dark caves
    between the shelves, reading
or perusing
    through steel rimmed spectacles.

The books he sold
    he sold reluctantly,
and yet to friends
    his generosity
could be superb,
    as if he wished to pay
a bonus on their company,
their conversation
    or their appreciation
of the pictures
    he would invite them to see.
"Bonnard did that of me."
    Yes, he had known Joyce,
and, so he said,
    Hemingway had been a customer.
    The place would echo
with the living dead
    when he spoke of them.

But now he's old
    his sight and friends
have gone.
    With skin the colour of the paper
he'd spent his eyes upon

he will emerge
(like some pale mollusc
    shrunk in its shell
and stranded by the tide)
    no longer to take pride
in the portrait by Bonnard
    or eagerly regard
the latest magazines
    from Rome or Paris.

What's left is safe enough
    within the mind;
but he's lost touch
    (the last sense of the blind).
Those friends who'd bring him news are dead,
    and so
his occupation gone
    he shuffles on
remembering a life
    crumbling about him.
Perhaps his chief regret
    he'd always meant to read
his Proust again, and yet
    he'd put if off, and put it off,
like dying, much too late.

SOUTHAMPTON WATER

The light vague, colourless
before sunrise, the ship sails
between grey shores, where street lamps,
like strung beads of light,
mark out the road
and make the only brightness.

Astern, watching the wake, white
on the flat steel line of sea,
and as dawn returns colour
to the body of the sky,
I remember those eyes
and subtleties of flesh
that set the detonators
for explosions in the blood,

and how, at every dawn
something is left behind.

TERMINI

There's something about main line stations,
those points of departure and areas
of unlimited goodbyes. Perhaps
it's the long perspective of rails,
or the dark puddles on the platforms
(like distillations of sad farewells)
or (like the eyes of same) the smoke dimmed
glass of those great halls. Then there's the mail
in trucks, waiting to be loaded, the steam
from platform urns or those wickered pigeons.
But I suspect it's all those goodbyes
that do it — there were those desperate,
long war-time ones, with intense kisses
and the last hasty fumblings of love
because it might be for always.
As it still may, for, though calmer now,
we're still not sure the one who will return
is leaning from the carriage window.

ENCOUNTER

She was there,
At the edge of the rise,
Sunlight glancing her hair.
Upright, lithe,
And barely breasting eighteen
She breathed the sharp air
Of an August morning,
The water drops like pearls
On the taut flesh
She dried after swimming.
Whose care what life
Hell is made in:
She was there
The sunlight -- water -- her hair;
While the tide,
That had washed the sand
To a rippled screed,
Moved on,
Whittling waists in the wood
Of breakwaters, scouring shells,
And, constant, grinding sea rocks
Into sand, eroding coasts,
And picking white bones
Clean of ulcerous flesh.

EDDIE'S AT THE MOVIES AGAIN

I'm at the old movies again,
safe in the warm dark
where the smoke serpents
into that shaft of light
the projector of dreams
where clichés fall
like rain in Ireland
and they even dress for breakfast.
Where girls keep their Marcel waves
unruffled in the jungle
and dresses tear
in just the right places.
Where the light's always on
in a home-town porch
like an entrance to a Greek temple,
and there's always appropriate music:
Somewhere Over the Rainbow for thinking
and *There's a Small Hotel* for love itself.
Where if you've got two girls
the brassy one dies,
but not before giving you
something to remember her by,
and where the murderer sends flowers
to your funeral and gets caught.
It's certainly such stuff
as dreams are made on.
A new opium of the people?
Not to worry —
with my girl beside me
and my hand in her blouse
I'll not lose touch.

RETURN

This is how the best reunions are,
No people, just places and memories
Which can't be held against the facts,
Only indulged and like the mountains, far
In the distance, fade into shades
Obscuring all harshness.

The bay deserted, to be recovered
By coots and plovers that hunt the shellfish,
The evening air broken by the shrill pipe
Of oyster catchers that have discovered
The approach of an intruder,
Which now is what I am.

Strange how strongly places evoke a past
As if it were yesterday, forgetful
That even the promises of such a warmth
Of flesh and affection as yours can't last,
Except in the mind, while concrete crumbles
And jetties lapse into the sea that frets them.

Yet there is the house, and from the stack
A drift of smoke, a light in the window
Of a room I can picture; but not enter.
Discretion the better part of memory, I'll turn back
Disturbing as I walk the small
Pale moths that fill the grass.

AMPURIAS (Home thoughts from abroad)

"it is not by our beliefs that we live but
by our habits" Radiguet

Like us they must have sat here
Looking out to a sea reflecting
An enamelled blue of sky, tired limbs
Absorbing the sun's warmth — certain things
Don't change in a millennium or two,
Like eternal vows that might last a lifetime.

The name tells us why they came,
Settled and built first a Greek, later
A Roman township, eventually
To be destroyed by barbarians
And silt, for ants to re-colonize
With their mindless if systematic culture.

Theirs was the pattern of streets,
Foundations, the need to occupy
Yet bring their own with them — even to
Their gods, always notoriously
Bad travellers. And how much — beyond
The obvious — did they fraternize
With the natives? And when they returned
What did they remember? Take with them?
What, if anything, lasted beyond
These stumps of walls and mosaic floors?
Lasts beyond the irrational moment,
The chemical violence forking through
The blood when the latent ape returns,
The barbarian in all of us?

At home the stubble's burning,
A rash of flames raw in late evening,
And in the suburbs the bonfire's gift,

37

A pall of smoke rich in the incense
Of burnt briar, marigolds and leaves:
The Autumnal rendering, the acid
Of it lingering in clothes and hair.

And after the cremation the tray
Of bits: coffin ash and the femor
Just recognizable. Scattered
At night the cold indifference of stars,
The folly, as always, to build to last.

In spite of the vows when will you
Recognize it love? Eventually
We all succumb to that deep eyed mistress
Who surpasses you. For there is peace
In the great breasts of her darkness,
Encompassed in the midnight of her thighs.

THE QUEST

"An individual must have some faith, otherwise he
must seek for it"

Chekov/*Three Sisters*

A reading of the *Quest del Saint Graal* suggested
that in each of the protagonists of the adventures
was the germ of a tragic character such as we find
in Shakespeare. Those who failed in The Quest
carried the cause of their failure within them, and
those who succeeded suffered such self-doubts as
could well have made them tragic figures: Lancelot
whose very qualities were his downfall; Bors whose
dogged persistence was assailed by intellectual
doubts and temptations; Gawain with his rigid
adherence to a courtly code and his impetuous
courage; Perceval whose simplicity was confused
with innocence; The Fisher King an archetypal
invalid; and Lancelot's son Galahad in the isolation
of his perfection. The following monologues
attempt to explore these themes.

LANCELOT

Numb fingers ease off my helmet
To brush the ice from my brow.
Before me the snow obliterates
All destinations; behind,
My tracks irredeemable
In the barren crispness.
I will not say I am not grateful
When the sun is high enough
To thaw the air, nor for
The occasional shelter of hostels
To ease the cramps of nights
Under the remoteness of stars
When the frost eats even
The metal of my armour.
Yet the blood is warm.

It is on those days when
Visited by failure,
The only sound the clash
Of ice-clad branches,
That I curse an ambition
I cannot fulfill,
While denied the blessings
Of a vocation for failure.
For the blood urges
Its own destinies, and when Spring
Renews the texture of life
With memories of a warmth
Which pressages my destruction,
And those scalding erruptions
Of a love I say I have forsworn,
Then I know
        — Can you hear me Guinevere?
I will do it again,
I will do it again.

BORS

Pride is not enough I say.
But where does such logic lead me?
Always to a choice between evils:
A brother's death or a maid's violation;
The rejection of either
My honour or my beatitude?
There is no need for hair shirts
When the burs are in the mind.

Yet the quest, like vanity, persists,
The body learning the lesser agonies
When Winter shrives the flesh,
Or Summer bastes me in a sweat
Sour in the oven of my armour.
It is what a man is proud of
That matters. Surely there is
Some merit in enduring?

GAWAIN

I was the first to go,
leaping up eager
for an adventure
I did not understand,
the quick flood of excitement
soon to congeal
in the blood of companions.

I tried to prove myself
the only way I knew how,
bolted in the armour
of an education
restrictive of all actions
except a crude butchery:
Act first and ask afterwards.

Well now I am asking,
having reached this estuary
where thin waters trickle
to the sea, the coarse grass
stitching such soil as there is,
the salt air rusting
already reddened arms.

Why did no one tell me
the rules had been changed?
Self denial is no creed
for a man who cannot say no.
Each step crushes the scoured
bleached husks of young crabs, deserted
in their thousands by the tide.

Another lesson in prodigality?
Too late. Will nothing wash
the taste of blood and salt from my mouth?

PERCEVAL

Above, in a crystal chip
of sky between the mountains,
the hawk pursues its innocence
in the death of others;
and I have heard of whales
betrayed by instinct
to return each Spring to bays
where knowing hunters wait
to spear them. Perceval,
a man cannot afford
to be simple, his purpose
betrayed by untutored
kindnesses, as morning air,
sharp on the lungs,
is blunted by the sun.
Innocence, as all things
with man, has to be attained.

FISHER KING

When the dawn seeps red
like a great wound
through the gauze of mist
on cold morning waters,
I am content to fish
my pain reduced
to a dull throb
as the batteries charge
for the next seizure.
Then, my wound wrenching open
and the full voltage
of agony galvanizing
my every nerve ending,
then, I call for rescue:
but not now.

There have been those who tried,
but failed, not knowing
the question without which
there could be no answer.
And if they had asked
could I have told them?
For what is achieved
by that which is destroyed
by its achievement?
As the true test of virginity
is its destruction,
as my truth is my pain
and as I am the source of my truth,
and as to be rescued
is to be without
the need for rescue,
so not now —

        the water's surface
undisturbed by the smooth
passage of fish, while
under the bark of still trees
insects inscribe their runes,
and the blood moves
through my unmoving body
as I fish, not sure what it is
I do not hope to catch.

GALAHAD

The vigil is ending,
    signalled by a lone
lark high flying
    somewhere in a sky
unstreaked by the dawn.
    Gradually,
the light
    sharpens images of day:
Still
    silhouettes of trees,
and lichened rocks
    betokening
a purity of air
    we would attain.

Today I am sure of success,
    the reward
of long nights
    in the darkness of forests,
of journeys
    across deserted plains,
having left
    my companions.
But the fragility of it!
    like some
cared for and precious bowl
    which one slip
will shatter in a second.

Is the end of the quest
    to exchange its burdens
for the burdens
    of its achievement?
for the ultimate loneliness
    of individual salvation,

where even one
    close as a father
is abandoned?
    Would we have it so?
or is that
    where the real choice lies?

NOTES

Labuan 1946

The year is significant not only because it is the year of the actual incident, but because this is (amongst other things) a poem about a certain aspect of time.

Report Back

"A Sentry on the Roman Wall felt he was at a terminus, the world's end" Andrew Young: "The New Poly-Olbion"

The Seafarer

This version is by no means a literal translation, but is slanted towards emphasizing what I feel is the principal theme of the poem, namely the struggle — the dichotomy — in man between the earthly and the spiritual. REPORT BACK is an attempt in S.F. terms to explore the same theme.